Take Charge of Your Career- Find Great Jobs, Negotiate Better Pay and Move Up the Corporate Ladder

Unconventional Techniques to Outfox Your Employer

Tejas Baxi

DISCLAIMER

The information provided within this book is for general informational purposes only. The author makes no representations or warranties, express or implied, about the completeness, accuracy, reliability, suitability or availability with respect to the information, ideas, techniques, or related graphics contained in this book for any purpose. Neither the author nor the publisher shall be held liable or responsible to any person or entity with respect to any loss or incidental or consequential damages caused, or alleged to have been caused, directly or indirectly, by any information contained herein. Every individual situation is different and the advice, strategies and techniques contained herein may not be suitable for your situation. Please use personal discretion in using the information in this book. In addition, you agree that any use of information contained in this book is at your own risk. All characters and entities are fictional. Any likeness to actual persons, either living or dead, is strictly coincidental.

Copyright © 2016 Tejas Baxi. All Right Reserved.

DEDICATION

I dedicate this book to my lovely wife and best friend, Jean, and to my wonderful son Arnav. You are my true inspiration and I feel blessed to have such a wonderful family.

Contents

Preface 5
Chapter 1 - The Hunt 12
Chapter 2 - The Reward 26
Chapter 3 - The Cage 45
Appendix A 56

PREFACE

Thank you for choosing this book from amongst the myriad of books available in the self-help aisle these days. By doing so, you have taken an important step towards taking charge of your career, moving up the corporate ladder and making lots of money along the way. Perhaps the first thing you will notice about this book is that it is rather petite. That is by design. I have focused on quality rather than quantity. Unlike other books that are hundreds of pages long but contain little in terms of effective, practical ideas, my goal is to be as direct, concise and to the point as possible while providing you with valuable tools that you can use from day one to get ahead in your career. To that end, everything discussed here is based on personal experience. I have successfully applied, tuned and perfected the techniques outlined in this book for over 12 years and have seen them deliver some amazing results, both during times of boom and also during periods of great economic distress (like the housing crash and the resulting recession of 2008). To give you some context and background and the motivation behind this book, I started my professional career in 2004 with a salary of about $38,000 a year. It took me a little over 2 years to realize that with my modest salary and the 2-3 percent raise that I was getting every year, not only was I never going to be able to afford the joys of a nice house or a luxury car but that it was going to be a struggle even to take a small vacation with my family every year. All the while, I saw the senior executives making absurd amounts of money. One example that I often recollect is the Executive Vice-President walking past my cubicle casually talking to one of the managers telling him how he had driven past a beautiful (multi-million) dollar vacation home in Vermont over the weekend and had decided to buy it. The fact that he could buy a multi-million dollar home more easily than I could afford to buy a new TV came as an eye-opener for me. I was working as hard as these corporate fat cats, perhaps even harder and yet, I was never going to get ahead in life unless something changed drastically. I was frustrated, angry and felt helpless at the sheer magnitude of pay disparity that I was seeing and experiencing in the corporate world. Fortunately, I decided to focus my anger and frustration on trying to find ways to change the status quo. If the system wasn't going to change, I had to change and change fast. I had to find ways to game the system and use the loopholes and weaknesses in the system to my advantage. And as I started taking calculated risks and trying out the very techniques that I am about to teach you, things started to change for me quite rapidly. In about 10 years, I saw my salary skyrocket from a little over $38,000 a year to well over $150,000 a year and that was not all. Adding all the benefits, I was now making well north of $200,000 a year. But the system had still not changed. It bothered me then and bothers me now. Millions of young professionals are still working their butt off, sacrificing the best years of their lives for companies that couldn't care less. Giving up valuable personal time as they work absurdly long hours hoping that their efforts get noticed and rewarded by a system that is inherently flawed and stacked against them and works only for the privileged few as they stuff themselves to the hilt with money and benefits. This book is dedicated to all those hard-working people. I hope that by sharing the techniques that have brought me so much success and money in such a short time, I can level the playing field a little bit and help others work around the system and get ahead in their careers just like I have. That is my motivation and the reason I wrote this book. However, before going any further, let me tell you a little bit about who this book is for, and more importantly, whom it is not for.

First and foremost, if you are looking for a quick and easy way to make money without hard-work then this is not the book for you and you might as well return it and start looking for spells and incantations at your local enchanters'. The techniques in this book require patience, discipline, hard work and a certain amount of risk-taking in order to yield results. Think of this book as one of many tools in your toolbox (albeit a very powerful and effective one) rather than some sort of magic wand that will make all your problems disappear.

Second, remember the age-old adage - "No risk, No Reward"? Well, that applies for a lot of what I am about to tell you. There is some element of risk-taking involved in using the techniques described here. So, if you are risk averse or your situation just doesn't allow you to take risks at this point, then this may not be the right book for you at this time.

Last but not the least, let me talk a little bit about the target audience for this book. I believe that the techniques in this book will best benefit professionals in 9-5, Full-Time, White Collar type jobs. That is not to say that others will not benefit from the contents. In fact, it is my hope that anyone who reads this book with an open mind, regardless of his or her profession, career level, industry or type of employment, will definitely derive some benefit from it. However, because the techniques in this book come from personal experience and interactions, mainly in White Collar, Full Time, 9-5 jobs, I just don't have enough experience or empirical data to judge the efficacy of these techniques when used by professionals in other kinds of jobs. They may be less (or more) effective but I just don't know enough and I think it is only fair that I disclose that up-front.

Now, with that out of the way, let me give you a quick idea about how the material is structured. You will find that the book is divided into 3 Chapters - "The Hunt", "The Reward" and "The Cage". The names reflect the actual steps in the job-hunting process and in exactly that order.

"The Hunt" is the very first chapter in the book and deals with the job-hunting process. It is the foundation on which the other two chapters are built. In order to get the maximum benefit out of this book, it is imperative that you read this chapter carefully and refer to it as many times as you need in order to understand the key concepts and apply them to your personal situation to the greatest extent possible

"The Reward" is the next chapter and addresses the

next phase after "The Hunt", i.e. after you have found a job and received a job offer. In this chapter, we discuss ways to negotiate the offer and how to make sure you squeeze every last dollar out of the offer and leave as little on the table as possible. I also introduce you to the TSM Number and how you can use it to evaluate any job offer and decide if you should negotiate or accept it.

The last chapter of the book is called "The Cage". After you have successfully completed "The Hunt" and maximized your offer or "The Reward", you are in "The Cage" aka your job and we discuss among other things, the art of differentiating yourself from your colleagues and standing out from the crowd using "Persistent Self-Marketing". We will also talk about how you can find out whether you are being rewarded appropriately for all your hard work and what to do if you are not.

Throughout the book you will see Cardinal Rules or CRs. I have tried to summarize the important concepts in each of the 3 chapters of the book into CRs. CRs are always in Bold font and have a Chapter Number and Rule Number associated with them so that you can quickly refer to them without having to read through the whole chapter. For example, CR-1/2 is read as Cardinal Rule - Chapter 1, Rule 2. Similarly if you come across CR-2/1, it would be read as Cardinal Rule - Chapter 2, Rule 1.

I hope you will find the contents of this book rewarding and will use the techniques outlined here to your maximum advantage.

CHAPTER 1 - THE HUNT

It all starts with the hunt. A lot of people will tell you about the "How" and the "Where" to hunt for a job. What they will not tell you (or just don't know) is the "When". The "When" as in "When to look for a new job" is far more important and much less understood than the "How" or the "Where" and forms the foundation for everything else in your career - So, let's ask the Sixty Four Million Dollar Question - "When should you start looking for a new job?"

The answer will become obvious once we discuss the two modes of Job Hunting. I like to call them "The Active Mode" and "The Passive Mode". Every job seeker, no matter what career level, industry or job type, always looks for a job in one of these two modes. The modes can be defined as follows

1. Active Mode - You are hunting for a job in the Active Mode when one of the following applies to you

a) You are about to lose your current job (or have already lost it) and as a result, have started looking for a new job.

OR

b) You have reached a level of frustration and dissatisfaction with your current job and even though your position may not be in imminent danger, you are actively looking for a new job.

Let's think about situations a) and b) for a second. Do you see a common theme between the two? The common theme in both situations (and by the way, this is true for every search conducted in the active mode) is that your decision to hunt for a new job is a reaction to an external set of events over which you have little or no control. Note the word "Reaction" because that is the principal difference between the "Active" and "Passive" modes. Also note that the type of event that caused you to start looking for a new job is not important. In other words, it doesn't matter whether you are looking for a new job because your company got acquired and the incoming management fired everyone or because your boss is an incompetent jerk with no appreciation for your work. The root cause or the "Initiating Event", seldom, if ever, impacts the outcome of the Active Mode.

By contrast, the "Passive Mode" can be defined as follows

2. Passive Mode - you are looking for a job in the passive mode when there is no pressing reason for you to do so. Your current position is secure. You are happy in your current job and your employer is happy with you. You might even be a rising star in the organization, maybe on a fast track for a promotion or that Employee of the Year Award. However, you are smart and prudent and realize that in today's corporate world there is no such thing as loyalty. The ruthless corporate culture is full of greed, backstabbing and companies more concerned about balance sheets and shareholders rather than their employees. Consequently, you also realize that fortunes can change in a matter of months, sometimes even weeks, and your dream job can become a horrendous nightmare often due to no fault of your own. You like to keep a trump card in your back pocket and are always open to a good opportunity. You keep in touch with friends, colleagues and professional contacts relatively regularly and also look at the job boards and websites every so often just in case you stumble upon an extraordinary opportunity. Note that although not very common, you could be looking for a job in the passive mode within the same company, maybe in a different unit, group or subsidiary within the organization.

Now that we have defined the two modes, let's compare them and see why the Passive mode is better and why you, the job seeker, should ALWAYS - look for a job in the Passive mode. This becomes our first Cardinal Rule (CR).

CR-1/1 - Always hunt for a job in the Passive Mode.

Trust me, you will be amazed at the results. In fact, you may be surprised (or not) when I tell you that most of the top executives in the corporate world - the VPs, SVPs, EVPs and the C-Suite folks, almost always hunt for jobs in the passive mode. So, why is the passive mode so much better and more importantly, why does it produce dramatically better results?

First and foremost, in the passive mode, time is on your side. Unlike the active mode, there is no pressure to find a job by a date certain or face the prospect of being unemployed. More time means less pressure, more flexibility and more options, which is a better deal for the job seeker.

Second, you have a much better negotiating position. Roger Fisher and William Ury introduced the term BATNA in their 1981 bestseller "Getting to Yes: Negotiating Without Giving In". BATNA stands for *"Best Alternative to a Negotiated Agreement"*. I will discuss the art of negotiating in more detail in Chapter 2 but for the purpose of our current discussion, BATNA can be described as the best alternative should your negotiations fail and you decide to "Walk Away" without making a deal. In order to negotiate effectively, it is very important to know your BATNA before you start the negotiation. Your BATNA determines how much leverage you have while negotiating, the risk you can afford to take and how hard you can push the other party during the negotiating process. For example, let's say that you are trying to sell your car for $10,000. Your neighbor notices the "For Sale" sign and makes you an offer of $9,000. However, another buyer, who is just passing by, sees your sign as well and offers you $8,500. You try and negotiate with the second buyer to see if he can top your neighbor's offer. Your BATNA while negotiating with the second buyer would be the original offer that you received from your neighbor ($9,000). Now, let's say you didn't have an offer from your neighbor. Can you guess what your BATNA would be in that case? Quite simply, your BATNA would be not to sell your car for $8,500 and hope that eventually another buyer shows up with a better offer.

Now that you understand the concept of BATNA, let's apply it to job hunting and more specifically, to the two modes that we just discussed earlier. Let's illustrate this with a fictitious example.

Scenario 1 - Our first fictitious character is a Software Engineer by the name of "Babie Souffle" who has recently lost his job as a result of his company relocating all technology related jobs overseas. Babie Souffle is unemployed and sitting at home. He is also desperately looking for a new job.

Question 1 - Can you guess which job-hunting mode he is using to look for his next job? If you answered "Active" - You are right.

Now, as it turns out, our friend, Mr. Souffle, gets a job offer from a local company. It's a great opportunity with a great company that's doing very well. He will still be a Software Engineer working in his area of expertise and it's a decent commute from home. Everything seems good except for one not so small problem. The new job pays $65,000/year with no bonus whereas at his previous job, Mr. Souffle used to make $75,000/year with an additional 10% bonus on top. Obviously, Mr. Souffle starts negotiating the job offer with his (potential) new employer trying to see if they can sweeten the pie a little bit.

Question 2 - Can you guess what is Babie Soufflé's BATNA in this negotiation?

The correct answer is - Stay unemployed and wait for another job that offers a better salary and bonus.

Scenario 2 - our second fictitious scenario involves a Project Manager named "Sam Kollander". Sam makes $90,000/year with a 15% bonus on top. He has been in this role for 2 years with his employer "Sunshine Tidy Bank". He is doing great in his role and everything seems to be going well for him but Sam is still looking for a job. He finds out from an ex-colleague that one of the local companies has an opening for a Senior Project Manager. Sam decides to go for it. He updates his resume and applies for the job.

Question 1 - What is Sam Kollander's job hunting mode? You are absolutely correct if you answered "Passive

Mode"

Question 2 - Let's say Sam aces the interview and gets a job offer from the new company. The new role offers a much better bonus of 20%. However, Sam asks for a better salary as well ($100,000/year) and in addition, asks for a $5,000 sign-on bonus. What is Sam's BATNA in this negotiation? His BATNA is...you got it... His current job with the $90,000/year base and 10% bonus.

You can clearly see the difference in BATNA between scenarios 1. and 2. Now that we realize the importance of looking for a job in the passive mode, I am going to provide some very specific time-based markers that you can follow in order to ensure that you are always looking for a position in the passive mode. The markers assume that you are currently employed.

CR-1/2 - Try and follow the Markers below. They will help you stick to the Passive Mode and should you ever wander away from it, they will guide you back.

- **Marker 1** - By the first anniversary at your current job, update your resume. For those of you, who have been at your job for several years and are reading this book for the first time, start immediately for you have long paid your dues and as soon as your resume has been updated, proceed to Marker 2 below.

• **Marker 2** - Between 12-18 months, spend at least 1 hour every week on a job board (or boards) of your choice. Look at job postings in your field. Research the salaries being offered in your area. Pay specific attention to positions that allow you to step up i.e. if you are working as a Software Engineer, look at Senior Software Engineer postings to see what kind of skills you will need to get there.

• **Marker 3** - If you need to pick up additional skills based on your research in Marker 2, start working on it. Give yourself at least 2-4 hours every week to learn and practice the new skills. You will be an expert before you know it. Even better if you can get your current employer to pay for that training (Of course, don't tell them of your plans or that you read this book!!)

• **Marker 4** - 18-24 months. Apply for new jobs and give at least 2 phone interviews (even better if you ace the phone screens and make it to the in-person interviews). Remember that you are hunting for a job in the passive mode so do not compromise and only apply for exceptional jobs that pay a lot more or allow you to step up. If asked during the interview about what you are looking for in terms of compensation, ask for at least 10% more than your current salary.

• **Marker 5** - 24 months onwards - pick up the pace. Spend at least 4-6 hours on job boards every week. Aim for at least 2 interviews a quarter till you find a new job or till you get a promotion in your current job. If you get a promotion, the clock resets and you go back to Marker 1.

CR-1/3 - While you are looking for a job in the Passive Mode, tell no one about it except your immediate family. Not your friends and certainly not your colleagues no matter how much you trust them. The time to disclose this information is only after you have accepted a new job offer and
1) Finalized a joining date at your new job.
and
2) Finalized a last day at your current job.

Even then, do not disclose the name of your new employer to anyone. No one needs to know. Spread the news too soon and you run the risk that someone may figure out where you are going and try and sabotage your new position. You have no way of knowing how jealous some of your colleagues may be and how far they may be willing to go to sabotage your career.

One last thing before we wrap up this chapter and move on to Chapter 2. Don't forget to do your homework before applying for any new job. Passive mode doesn't mean being sloppy, careless or negligent. There is nothing more depressing than getting a new job and finding out that it is not what you expected and worse still, that you had all the information available to you right at your fingertips but you did not do your homework. I speak from personal experience. Many years ago, I made the mistake of applying for a job (in the passive mode) with a prominent healthcare company. It looked like a great opportunity - I was to be the Enterprise Architect with a direct shot at being a VP in a few years. There was a great sign-on bonus and a decent step-up in salary. I aced the interview and believed all the stories that the management told me. I should have done my own research about this company but did not and ended up accepting their offer. On my first day at work, I came across an email from the

CEO congratulating the employees for keeping the company on-track to meet it's yearly goal - which was to lose no more than 11 million dollars that year. Yes, that was actually the goal the management was aiming for. On doing a little online research about the company, I quickly learnt that the company had laid off a large chunk of it's workforce barely 6 months earlier and the guy who had my job was laid off at that time as well. It made me sick to the pit of my stomach to see how badly the company was doing and that everything that I had been told during the interview was at best a misrepresentation and at worst a lie. However, it was my mistake that I did not try to fact check the information that was presented to me during the interview process. I could have avoided this costly mistake in my career had I just spent a few hours researching this company online before accepting the job. There was enough information out there in the public domain that would have raised (more than a few) red flags and made me run for the door. To avoid making the same mistake that I made, I strongly recommend that you search for the following pieces of information about a prospective employer before applying for a job (especially, if you do not know what the company does and have no information about the health of their business or their finances).

CR-1/4 - Never apply or accept a job with a company without doing due diligence and searching for any available information (positive or negative) in the public domain.

> 1. Look at reviews on job boards and review sites like "www.indeed.com" and "www.glassdoor.com". I try and look at the number of negative reviews and read each one of them to see if there are any common threads that emerge from them.
>
> 2. Do a search in your favorite search engine (I prefer Google but to each one their own) for any recent layoffs that the company may have had. Remember to look through at least the first 2 pages of the search results to make sure you did not miss anything. While you are at it, try some other keywords as well. So, for example if you are looking for information on a company called "ABC Investments", you could use search terms like *ABC Investments + Layoffs, ABC Investments + Losses and ABC Investments + Revenue*

3. Last but not the least, go the company webpage and look for any financial information that they may have published. For publicly traded companies, this can usually be found under "Investor Relations" or "About Us". Some companies also provide a separate link for their financial results broken down by years or sometimes even by quarters. Look through the Prior Year and the Current Year results to see if the company is beating or missing revenue targets. Is it profitable or are the losses increasing? Also remember to check their forecast for next year in case it's publicly available. You want to avoid joining companies that are shrinking and cutting their revenue and growth forecasts because eventually all that translates into pay and/or benefit cuts and layoffs.

CHAPTER 2 - THE REWARD

Chapter 1 discussed "The Hunt". That forms the foundation for this chapter so feel free to refer back to it if you need to. Now, let's say you are looking for a job in the Passive Mode. You have followed all the steps in Chapter 1, done your due diligence, aced the interviews and just received an offer from a really great employer. Congratulations, you obviously did very well in the hunt but there is still a long way to go before we can claim success. How do you know that you are getting a good deal? Is this the absolute best offer that you could have got? Are you leaving a lot on the table? The answer is that you really can't tell any of this just by looking at the offer. However, if there is one thing you can bet on, it's this - the offer that you just received was not the absolute best that you could have got. There is always room for negotiation and more importantly, there is always more money on the table. Our aim in this chapter is to help you find as much of it as possible and help you squeeze every last penny out of the offer before accepting it.

If you really think about it, hunting for a job is no different than looking for a car except you will probably change your job sooner than your car. When you are out car shopping and find one that you want to buy, what is the next thing that you do? Negotiate a good price, right? You wouldn't pay MSRP for a car unless it's a low inventory, highly sought after luxury automobile like a Land Rover or a Porsche. The same reasoning applies to a job offer. Unless you get an amazing offer from the Land Rovers and Porsches of the Corporate World, so to say - and I am talking about companies like Apple, Google, Facebook and Amazon (and a handful of others), you should never accept the first offer extended to you.

CR-2/1 - Never accept the first offer made to you by a

company. Ask for some time to consider it and then decline it diplomatically asking for more goodies within reason. By Goodies, I mean Pay/Stock/Sign-on Bonus or any other benefit that is important to you. The TSM number discussion later in the chapter will help you compare benefits in the offer with your current job and help you decide when to accept an offer.

Now, I know this goes against conventional wisdom and there are tons of people out there who still believe that saying no to a job offer may cause you to lose the job but that is simply not the case, especially in a good job market and as long as you play your cards right. Let me tell you a little secret that companies don't want you to know. Many companies compensate the recruiting teams based on how much money they were able to save while filling an open position. In other words, your recruiter gets a bonus if they get you to accept a lower offer. The lower you go, the more bonuses they make. Now, to be fair, there are other factors at play too. There are overall company policies, compensation bands and guidelines on where companies want most of their new hires to start.

Remember though, these are just guidelines and there is always more money on the table for those who can find it. Let me illustrate this with a real life example from one of my previous jobs. We needed to fill two Senior Level Programmer positions. Both positions got approved for a base salary of upto $140,000 per year. We went through the interview process and had a lot of trouble finding the right candidates for these positions. Eventually though, we did find two really talented folks and decided to make them an offer. Now, remember that by this time we had wasted over three months interviewing many candidates for these positions. We were desperate (and I mean really, really desperate) to fill these roles and fill them pronto. Judging from our desperation, you would think that we would have made these candidates a really good offer, right? But that is not how the system works. Between fairness and greed, greed always triumphs in the corporate world. In this case, we ended up offering both candidates a starting salary of $105,000/year. This was $35,000 less than the maximum amount that the positions were approved for. As it often happens in these situations, it was up to the individual candidates to negotiate (or not to negotiate) a better deal. One of them did not negotiate a lot and ended up accepting an (revised) offer of $110,000/year while the other candidate negotiated much harder and got a (significantly higher) revised offer with an annual salary of $120,000/year. Now, think about this for a minute. Candidate 2 was able to make $10,000 more than Candidate 1 for the same role just because he negotiated harder and declined the initial offer. Actually, he ended making quite a bit more than that because many benefits are based on the base salary. So, for example, if both positions had a 5 percent 401k match, Candidate 1 got 5% of 110,000 or $5,500/year while Candidate 2 got 5% of 120,000 or $6,000/year. In addition, these positions also had an additional annual bonus of 10% of the base salary payable at the end of the year. Candidate 2 ended up making more money there too, $12,000 vs. $11,000 for Candidate 1. So, by the end of the year, Candidate 2 actually made $11,500 more than Candidate 1. Not bad, right? But this was just one job. As they both progress through their careers, this difference keeps getting more amplified. Assuming that both candidates change their jobs every 3 years and Candidate 2 negotiates $15,000 more than the offer every time, he will make over $289,000 more than Candidate 1 over a 10 year period. Check out **Appendix A** at the end of the book for the detailed calculations.

This scenario tends to happen quite a lot during a strong job market, especially in hard to fill roles. Companies open positions, they are unable to find the right candidate for a whole host of reasons and get really desperate. Often, there are signs that you can watch for during the interview process. If you are lucky, your interviewer may slip up and say something that gives you an indication of just how desperate they really are. If that happens, use that information to your advantage and negotiate aggressively when you do get the job offer.

CR-2/2 -Listen for any clues that the interviewers may inadvertently give you during the interview process. Use them to your advantage if you get an offer. Most of the times the clues will come in the form of minor slip-ups like - "We have been interviewing for this position for a while now" or "We have been finding it hard to fill this role". If you hear these statements or variations thereof, you should translate them to "We are really desperate to fill this position" and should you be offered the job, use this information to

aggressively negotiate a great deal.

So far we have talked a lot about the job offer and negotiating a great deal. But what are the ingredients of a good offer? What are the different benefits that are available? Let's discuss these different benefits in more detail. Remember, not every job may offer all the benefits listed below but it's good to be aware of them nevertheless. Also, this is by no means an exhaustive list of every single benefit out there but covers the most common ones that you find in the vast majority of jobs.

1. Base Salary - regardless of what other benefits matter to you, this is the most important thing to watch for in any job offer. As we discussed earlier, many of the other benefits are based off of your base salary so a higher base means higher benefits and a higher pay package. Several sites have popped up that allow you to search for pay by industry, job type and even by a specific employer (i.e. www.payscale.com, www.glassdoor.com, www.indeed.com to name a few of them.)

2. 401k Match - Many companies will put additional money into your retirement account as long as you contribute a certain amount of money yourself. This company matching can be anywhere from 1% to 7% of your salary though very few go over 5% these days and most companies will probably match around 2-3%. As you can see, a higher base means more money in your retirement account as well.

3. Sign-On Bonus- this is perhaps the most undervalued and under utilized of benefits. Because of the housing crisis and the resulting recession of 2008-2009, most people have just stopped asking for a sign-on bonus let alone trying to negotiate one. However, this is also one of the easiest benefits to negotiate. From an employer's perspective, it is much easier to pay a sign-on bonus and close the deal than to negotiate benefits like bonus or stocks, because those would generally need approvals from Finance, Legal and Senior Management. Most sign-on bonuses get paid out within the first 30, 60 or 90 days of your joining the company and require you stay a certain amount of time in the job (commonly 1 yr.). If you leave before a year, you are generally required to pay back the sign on bonus that you received (although, if you stayed for 10 or 11 months and decided to leave, most companies won't bother coming after you unless it's a significant sign-on bonus running into several tens of thousands of dollars. It's cheaper to let you get away with a modest sign-on than pay massive legal fees to lawyers to come after you). In every job that I have accepted, I have always asked for a sign-on and have never been refused it, which is why it never hurts to ask. The worst that can happen is the company will say no but more often than not, you will end up walking away with several thousand dollars of additional money in your pocket.

4. Annual Bonus - Many employers offer an annual bonus that is calculated as a percentage of the base salary and paid out at the end of the year. The calculations can vary widely, from the simple to dizzying and mind numbingly complex. The simplest kind is a flat bonus (i.e. 5% of your annual salary at the end of the year as long as the company meets or beats their targets for that year). Then there are companies that make this calculation excruciatingly complex (i.e. Take into account the overall company profitability, the unit or group's performance and also the individual's performance and use a secret or arcane formula to calculate the bonus which is then paid out at the end of the year). This is another benefit that is directly tied to and is impacted by your Base Salary.

5. Profit Sharing (PS) - Some employers, albeit very few and a rapidly dwindling bunch, include PS as a part of the overall pay package. The way PS works is that for every year that the company beats it's numbers and makes a profit, every eligible employee gets an additional amount of money (mostly between 5 to 10% of the base salary) paid out and deposited into their retirement account. Note that this is in addition to the 401k match. Always check and see if your company has a PS program and if your position is eligible.

6. Stocks - Many positions, especially as you go higher up the corporate ladder, often come with stock units. Be extremely careful about what you are signing up for. There can be serious tax implications based on the kind of stocks you are offered. Generally, I prefer Restricted Stock Units or RSUs. These units become equivalent to the common stock of the company upon vesting and have a value upon vesting regardless of the actual price of the stock. Of course, the higher the stock price, more the value of your reward. In contrast, while many companies tout stock options as a benefit, I do not recommend that you give them as much weight since they only represent the right to purchase a unit of stock at a certain price, often at a discounted price. You still have a vesting period and only make money if the price of the stock is above your strike price after the vesting period. It's often hard to figure out the true value of these options at the time that you get them. They can be worth quite a bit or they could be worth nothing by the time they vest. Unlike RSUs, which are always worth something after vesting as long as the company is in business, the value of Stock Options is hard to predict and that is why I do not like to count them as an assured or tangible benefit. Also, here's my other pet peeve with Stock Options. Employees work their butt off for the company and get paid a salary for their hard work. They already lose a significant chunk of it as taxes. How is it a benefit if they have to once again dip into their savings to buy stocks and hope that in several years time, that money that they have invested will be worth something? And that is why I recommend that you ask for RSUs rather than Stock Options when negotiating a job offer. Make sure you take some time to learn about the differences between Stock Options and RSUs. There is a lot of information available online for free.

7. Insurance - When I say insurance, I use it to include the Medical, Dental and Vision insurance plans offered by employers. A bad health insurance plan is like a Trojan horse. It can sneak in unnoticed with your job offer and has the potential to not only negate all the other benefits in a job but also cause significant financial and psychological damage to you and your family. Make sure that you ask for details about all the insurance plans that your (potential) new employer offers. Don't settle just for the summary but ask for a detailed plan prospectus that explains all medical conditions that are covered and the ones that aren't and the coverage that the plan offers. The detailed plan will also give you a good idea of your co-pay, deductible and annual out of pocket maximum expenses. Compare the new plan with the one you have at your present job in order to understand the full financial impact of accepting the job offer. In Chapter 1, I told you a little about how I made the mistake of joining a prominent healthcare company without doing due diligence. Among the various things that I did not research was their Health Insurance plan. I assumed, rather naively of course, that being a healthcare company, my new employer probably had a really great healthcare plan. I couldn't have been more mistaken. When my son started having medical problems and we needed a lot of tests and specialist visits, I realized that my plan barely covered anything and within a short span of a few months, I had accumulated several thousand dollars worth of debt due to the medical bills which more than negated any gains that I had made in my base salary or bonus by accepting the job. I share this painful experience so that you may learn from my mistakes and not make the same mistake that I made.

8. Miscellaneous Benefits - I am clubbing anything that we haven't covered so far under this category. Benefits in this category can include Work-Life balance, Vacation and Time-off, Life Insurance, flexibility to work from home, etc. Not all of them matter to everyone but they can be very important based on your personal situation.

So far in this chapter, we have talked about different things - the need to negotiate, never accepting the very first offer an employer makes, looking for signs of desperation from the employer during the job interview. We have also looked at some of the common benefits that companies tend to offer these days. Now, let's build on all that and weave this together into something more concrete. Wouldn't it be wonderful if there were an easy way to evaluate a job offer? What if there was a way to quantify a job offer and know with a high degree of accuracy whether you should accept it or decline it and try and negotiate a better one. Well, I am happy to tell you that there is a way to do just that. Let me introduce you to the concept of the TSM Number. TSM stands for "There's Something Missing". This is a concept that I have developed and refined over the years using personal experience as well as feedback from a select few who have tried this technique out. The TSM number is a unique way to evaluate a job offer based on the 8 benefits that we discussed earlier. The way it works is that we first assign each of these 8 benefits a numeric value based on their relative importance from a financial perspective and long term career potential. Next we compare each of these benefits in the (new) Job Offer (JO) with the Existing Job (EJ). We split the benefits into two groups. The first group consists of benefits where their monetary value in JO > EJ. In other words, this group contains the benefits that are better in the job offer than the current job. This group becomes the "YAY Group". The second group contains the benefits where their value in EJ > JO. In other words, this group contains the benefits that are worse (or much less in monetary value) in the job offer compared to the existing job. This becomes the "NAY Group". Add the values in the YAY group to get the YAY Number. Then do the same for the NAY group to get the NAY Number. The TSM number is the difference between the YAY Number and the NAY number. If a benefit exists in only the

JO or the EJ but not in both, then assign a zero value to it where it is missing so that you can generate the YAY and NAY Numbers in such situations.

CR-2/3 - The TSM Number = YAY Number - NAY Number.

A positive TSM number implies that the combined financial value of benefits in the job offer that you received is better than your current job and hence you could accept this offer without re-negotiating it. The higher the TSM Number the better is your offer compared to your present job.

On the other end, a Negative TSM number means - "There's Something Missing in the Job Offer" and you should re-negotiate the offer. Once you re-negotiate and get a better offer, recalculate the TSM number again to see if it's positive, your aim is to renegotiate an offer until you have an offer with a positive TSM number.

There is one more scenario to consider here i.e. what happens when the TSM Number is zero. This happens when the YAY Number is exactly equal to the NAY Number. In such cases, you are right on the fence. Your offer is very close to your existing job in terms on money and impact on your long-term career. In this scenario, use your judgment and discretion to decide if you should accept the offer or renegotiate it. My recommendation would be to renegotiate even though the offer is close in value to your current job. After all, why would you want to move to a new job if there is no net gain in doing so?

Now that we have discussed the TSM Number and how to calculate it, let's assign numeric values to each of the 8 benefits discussed earlier. I recommend that you do not alter these values or switch them between benefits, even if you may not agree with my assignment. These assignments are not based on a benefit's short-term impact but the ability of the benefit to have a positive monetary impact on your long-term career as well as your ability to negotiate really positive offers in the future. I have adjusted and refined this matrix over many years to make it efficient and accurate.

Benefit Values (In Descending Order of Significance)

	Benefit Name	Points
1.	Base Pay	3
2.	Annual Bonus	2
3.	401k Match	1.5
4.	Health Insurance	1.5
5.	Profit Sharing	1
6.	Sign-on Bonus	0.5
7.	Stocks (RSUs Only)	0.25
8.	Miscellaneous	0.25

Let's illustrate this with some examples.

Scenario 1 - The Job Offer (JO) has a higher Base Pay (Benefit 1. from above) than the Existing Job (EJ) but the EJ is better in terms of every other benefit.

YAY No. = 3 (Value for Base Pay from Table 1.)

NAY No. = 7 (Sum of values for the rest of the benefits from Table 1. i.e. 2 + 1.5 + 1.5 + 1 + 0.5 + 0.25 + 0.25)

TSM No. = - 4 (3-7)

Overall Conclusion: Negative TSM Number. Renegotiate the offer

Scenario 2 - The Job Offer (JO) has a higher Base Pay (Benefit 1) and Annual Bonus (Benefit 2) and a better Sign-On Bonus (Benefit 6) than the Existing Job (EJ) but the EJ is better in terms of other benefits.

YAY No. = 5.5

NAY No. = 4.5

TSM No. = 1 (5.5 - 4.5)

Overall Conclusion: Positive TSM Number. Ok to accept the offer.

Scenario 3 - The Job Offer (JO) has a higher Base Pay (Benefit 1) and Annual Bonus (Benefit 2) but the EJ is better in terms of all other benefits.

YAY No. = 5

NAY No. = 5

TSM No. = 0 (5 - 5)

Overall Conclusion: Use your discretion. Personal recommendation - Renegotiate the offer.

CR-2/4 - A positive TSM Number = Accept the offer
        A negative TSM Number = Renegotiate the offer

A zero TSM Number = Use your judgment renegotiation recommended

This brings us to the end of this Chapter. So far we have discussed "The Hunt" or looking for a job and "The Reward" or negotiating the best pay and benefits in any potential new job. In the next chapter, we will discuss "The Cage" which refers to the time you spend at work and I will show you techniques that you can employ to maximize your earning potential and accelerate your career growth.

CHAPTER 3 - THE CAGE

The Cage refers to the place where we spend at least a third of our day, often much more than that. In other words, "The Cage" refers to the workplace. Some of you might say that calling the workplace "The Cage" is perhaps a little too harsh. Maybe, but let's face it, where would you rather be - vacationing on some tropical island by the beach sipping your favorite cocktail or at work slogging away for some employer that doesn't really care whether you exist or not, as long as the job gets done and they make a profit. Most of us spend a big chunk of our adult life at work, arguably our prime years. We work our butt off and hope that our hard work gets noticed and appropriately rewarded. Sometimes that happens, often times it doesn't. There are two main reasons why employees can feel unappreciated and under compensated.

1. The employer is cheap, unappreciative and has a sweatshop mentality. The management doesn't care about the worker bees. All that matters is the profit and even that is distributed amongst the senior management and rarely shared with the middle and lower rung workers. If you are stuck with such an employer, start looking for a job in the passive mode immediately. Follow the techniques that you learnt in Chapters 1 & 2 and say Ciao as soon as you find something better.

2. The employees are working hard and while they may assume that the management is aware of their hard work, the management is often obtuse and/or preoccupied with other initiatives and projects. In this case, the oversight is not deliberate or intentional and there are steps that you, the employee, can take to highlight your work. We will discuss the concept of "Persistent Self Marketing" (or PSM) as well as the "1

Minute Water Cooler Conversation" technique that will allow you to market yourself more effectively to your manager and to senior management. It will also allow you to use every interaction with your superiors to your advantage.

Let's talk about the "1 Minute Water Cooler Conversation" technique first. Why do I call it that? Simple, because it is exactly that. Ask yourself this question - How many times have you run into your VP or SVP or someone influential from Senior Management in the Kitchen, at the Water Cooler or in the Cafeteria waiting to be rung up at the check-out register? And how many times have you used that quick 1 or 2 minute casual conversation to market yourself or highlight your achievements to them? Each of these interactions is an invaluable opportunity for you to market yourself to the people who make the real decisions in the organization, the people who really matter in terms of you getting that raise, or extra bonus or the promotion that you are looking for. It's a chance for you to differentiate yourself from the crowd and leave a positive lasting impression. Do that every time with every Senior Manager you run into and you will be surprised at the results. However, that is not how a vast majority of these interactions go. Let's take an example of a wasted opportunity.

Our fictitious character Jim is working hard on a highly visible Infrastructure Upgrade project. He runs into the Senior Vice-President (SVP) in the kitchen. The interaction goes something like this

SVP: Hey Jim. How are you doing?

Jim: Great. How are you doing? How was your weekend?

SVP: Good. We had a party and the kids enjoyed it.

Jim: Oh, that's great.

SVP: Yes. Well, see you later.

Jim: Bye.

That was a wasted opportunity, don't you think? There was nothing in that conversation that made Jim stand out professionally. In a few minutes, the SVP will have probably forgotten that the conversation ever happened and Jim would have squandered away an invaluable interaction with someone very influential and important whom he doesn't get a chance to interact with everyday.

Instead, let's say that Jim read this book and decided to

try the "1 Minute Water Cooler Conversation" technique. Here's how that same interaction would go.

SVP: Hey Jim. How are you doing?

Jim: Great. We are just wrapping up testing for our Infrastructure Upgrade project. We found some issues in testing but I made sure we fixed all of them so that we stay on track for a successful delivery.

SVP: That's great. Thank you for all your hard work.

Jim: Oh, no problem. Thank you for giving me the opportunity to work on this important project.

SVP: No problem. Take Care

Jim: Bye.

What just happened? Jim used the opportunity to his advantage. Instead of idle talk, he marketed his hard work and differentiated himself from others who may be working equally hard (maybe even harder) on that same project. When Jim is competing for that promotion and his name is one of many in the ring and the SVP has to make a decision, guess whose name will be picked for that promotion? Obviously, someone that the SVP perceives as being a hard worker and someone he has interacted with directly even if for only a minute or two. Perception is everything and if you follow my technique religiously you will be the management's darling. You will have built a perception that you are a loyal hard working employee who cares deeply about the company and loves to deliver results and once you have built that perception, good things will start happening to your career very quickly.

CR-3/1-Use the "1 Minute Water Cooler Conversation" Technique when you run into Senior Management at the Water Cooler, Cafeteria, Kitchen, in the Hallway or even at the Christmas Party. Try not to have empty meaningless conversations. Use the opportunity to market yourself. This Self-Marketing will produce amazing results in the long run.

The "1 Minute Water Cooler Conversation" technique leads us into a broader conversation about Persistent Self Marketing (PSM). I used the term "Technique" to describe PSM but it's really much more than that. It is, what I like to call, a work way of life. It's something you practice, live and breathe when you are at work. Don't just limit self-marketing to the 1 or 2 min cooler conversations. Every time you have a one-on-one with your manager, talk about your achievements (since the last meeting). Be prepared for the meeting. It doesn't have to be hours of preparation, 10-15 minutes will do. Once again, if you do this religiously, week after week, month after month, not only will you be successful in marketing yourself but more importantly, you will be able to mold your image in the eyes of the management the way you want before someone else does.

There is one more important topic that is worth discussing here. Whether you feel unappreciated due to reasons 1. or 2., it is important to find out exactly where you are in terms of your Base Salary relative to your peers in the company. Many of the larger companies publish salary ranges on the company intranet. If you can't find this information on the intranet, try and check with your manager or HR to see if this information is available to the employees in a different format. Look through the document. If it lists the median salary for your level, make a note of it and compare your salary with the median. If your salary is less than 90 percent of the median salary, you are underpaid and if it is less than 80 percent, you should be outraged at the disparity. Not only does the lower salary mean a lower overall pay package (after all, as we discussed in Chapter 2., most of your benefits are based off your base salary) but it can also hurt you during the promotion process. One of the inputs into promoting an employee, believe it or not, is their salary and where they are in the salary band. Companies do not like big changes to the median salary and try to make sure that most of the employees fall within 90%-110% of the median salary for their grade. Once an employee starts to go outside the 110% marker, he or she becomes a good candidate for a promotion as long as they are a consistent high performer and in good standing with the management. Rather than impacting the median for the current grade, promoting them puts them in a different (higher) grade with a higher median where they will not move the median salary up (in fact, they may end up moving the median salary in that band lower). Bring up the issue of your lower salary with your manager to see if the company can do a one-time adjustment or correction to bring you closer to the Median. If your manager or HR agrees, that's great. If they can't or won't, don't be afraid to voice your disappointment (politely and diplomatically, of course) and ask them if they can use your annual performance review as an opportunity to compensate you appropriately in other ways to make up for the shortfall in your salary. Conveying your disappointment does two things

- A. You have let your manager (and HR) know that you are aware of the fact that you are being underpaid. That prevents them from trying any tricks or playing politics with you, either on purpose or inadvertently, to aggravate you further.
- B. Ever heard the saying, "The Squeaky Wheel gets the Grease"? Well, that applies here as well, even if you do not get an immediate salary adjustment or correction. As long as you are a consistent high performer, the management will try and find ways to make you feel valued. This can take the form of higher annual pay increases compared to your peers (i.e. You get a 5% raise when others are getting a 3% raise), a larger annual bonus or stock units (or all of the above if you are lucky and play your cards well).

CR-3/2-Find out the Median Salary for your grade and compare it with your salary. If you are making

less than 90% of the median salary, take the matter up with your manager. Make sure you let them know that it is a big deal and not just a small inconvenience. If your manager is unwilling or unable to adjust it and bring it closer to the Median, ask them if you can be compensated in other ways to make up for this shortfall.

Give your company about 6 months to try and fix the discrepancy (or at least ask for a definite timeline on when and how they plan to address the issue). At the end of six months or the timeline that you were provided by the company, if you are still not satisfied with the steps taken then start looking for a job in the passive mode.

That brings us to the end of this chapter and also this book. In conclusion, if I could sum up everything that we have discussed so far in just a few sentences, I would say this - Fight for yourself. Don't ever stop. There will be successes and there will be failures but if you follow my techniques, a lot more of the former rather than the latter. Along the way, you will meet people who will try and discourage you. You will meet recruiters and HR associates who will tell you that you are asking for too much money in that new job or that you are not qualified for that position that you want to step-up to. Don't listen to them. Remember that no one owes you anything nor do you owe anything to anyone. It is a pure business transaction and everyone wants to move up the corporate ladder, make more money and provide a better life for themselves and their families. There is nothing wrong with that and nothing to feel guilty about or apologize for. Hopefully, this book has added value to your career and will take you closer towards achieving your dreams and most importantly making money, a lot more of it. All the best.

APPENDIX A

In Chapter 2 (Page 25), I talked about a situation at one my previous jobs where we hired 2 Senior Level Programmers at vastly different salaries based on how hard they negotiated. To recollect, they were both offered a starting salary of $105,000/yr. Candidate 1 negotiated $5,000 more and was hired at a Base Salary of $110,000/yr. while Candidate 2 negotiated $15,000 more and was hired at a Base Salary of $120,000/yr. Let us extrapolate these numbers, make some assumptions and see how the two candidates stack up financially after 10 Years. Let's make the following assumptions.

1. Both candidates switch jobs every 3 years. At the end of 10 years both candidates would have switched jobs 3 times and would be on Job Number 4.

2. Let's assume that every time they switch jobs, they look for a job in the passive mode and each candidate gets an offer with 10% higher base salary than the job they are leaving.

3. Candidate 2 consistently negotiates harder than candidate 1. So, every time they switch, candidate 2 negotiates $15,000 more than the salary he is first offered while candidate 1 negotiations $5000 more than the offer (Just as they did when they got the jobs at my previous employer in our discussion in Chapter 2).

4. Annual raises in Salary are always 2% and the additional benefits for purposed of this discussion are 401k Match at 5% of Base Salary and Annual Bonus at 10% of Base Salary.

5. All amounts are rounded off to the nearest dollar.

Benefits	Candidate 1 ($)	Candidate 2 ($)	Net Gain Candidate 2 ($)
Year 1 (Job 1)			
Base	110,000	120,000	10,000
401k	5,500	6,000	500
Bonus	11,000	12,000	1,000
Year 1 Total			11,500
Year 2 (2% Raise)			
Base	112,200	122,400	10,200
401k	5,610	6,120	510
Bonus	11,220	12,240	1,020
Year 2 Total			11,730

Year 3 **(2% Raise)**			
Base	114,444	124,848	10,404
401k	5,722	6,242	520
Bonus	11,444	12,485	1,041
Year 3 Total			**11,965**
Year 4 (Job 2)			
Offer **(10% Raise)**	125,888	137,333	
Base **(Negotiated)**	130,888	152,333	21,445
401k	6,544	7,617	1,073
Bonus	13,089	15,233	2,144
Year 4 Total			**24,662**
Year 5			

(2% Raise)			
Base	133,506	155,380	21,874
401k	6,675	7,769	1,094
Bonus	13,351	15,538	2,187
Year 5 Total			**25,155**
Year 6 (2% Raise)			
Base	136,176	158,488	22,312
401k	6,809	7,924	1,115
Bonus	13,618	15,849	2,231
Year 6 Total			**25,658**
Year 7 (Job 3)			
Offer (10% Raise)	149,794	174,337	

Base (Negotiated)	154,794	189,337	34,543
401k	7,740	9,467	1,727
Bonus	15,479	18,934	3,455
Year 7 Total			**39,725**
Year 8 (2% Raise)			
Base	157,890	193,124	35,234
401k	7,895	9,656	1,761
Bonus	15,789	19,312	3,523
Year 8 Total			**40,518**
Year 9 (2% Raise)			
Base	161,048	196,986	35,938
401k	8,052	9,849	1,797

Bonus	16,105	19,699	3,594
Year 9 Total			**41,329**
Year 10 (Job 4)			
Offer (10% Raise)	177,153	216,685	
Base (Negotiated)	182,153	231,685	49,532
401k	9,108	11,584	2,476
Bonus	18,215	23,169	4,954
Year 10 Total			**56,962**
Total Year 1 To Year 10			**289,204**

*Candidate 2 makes $289,204 more than Candidate 1 over a 10-year period.

Notes

www.ingramcontent.com/pod-product-compliance
Lightning Source LLC
Chambersburg PA
CBHW070401190526
45169CB00003B/1054